The Unpartnered Wife

by

Karen Moulton

All rights reserved.
Copyright © 2016 by Karen Moulton.

No part of this manuscript may be reproduced or transmitted in any form or by any means, electronic or mechanical, including photocopying, recording, or by any information storage and retrieval system, without permission in writing from the author.

ISBN 9780692764671
LCCN 2016913120

Printed by Village Books in Bellingham, WA.

For James

*For Ted and Jeanette, whose care and nourishment
sustained me*

For Betsy and Bill, for their steadfast bedside devotion

Table of Contents

Dear Reader 7
Parallel Universe 8
Far Removed 10
April Fools 11
Evanescence 12
Winter Walk 13
The Unpartnered Wife 14
What I Carry 15
If Only He Could Say 16
My Baby 17
Close 18
Coralled 19
Threshold 20
Tortured Sonnet 21
Satisfied 22
Future Memories 23
What the Brain Knows 24
So Much For Being Good 25
The Day for Lovers 26
Happy Hour 27
Tapestry 28
Still 29
Leaving Me 30
Gone 31
One More Day 32
Before My Eyes 34
Feed Your Head 35
Voice 36
Like a Dream 38
Remaining Faithful 39
Is Sleep Not a Rehearsal 40
What I Hold Onto 41
Rise Up 42
The Art of Healing 43
Exposed 44

Dear Reader

This poem wants you to see how a woman
feels when she flies away from her mate,
how her heart shatters into bits of memory
she collects and glues together, like a jigsaw
puzzle you want to keep whole, but so loosely
held together that every phone call when he isn't
able to talk to her, loses another piece.

This poem wants you to know what it's like when one
day away from him adds to another until it's months
away. This time does not fly by. This time
is agonizingly slow, as if the clock hands
are moving through hot tar, black and blistering,
so heavy on her skin. Here is the darkness
this woman wears. Feel the weight of it.

This poem doesn't want to use words
like heartbroken, heartsick. This poem needs
your help. It wants you to bring your memories,
your experiences to it to understand, to feel
her pain, to endure the wait. It needs you to come
closer, to hold your fingertip over the flame.

Parallel Universe

You see me dancing at Sloppy Joe's bar,
fall in love with my long blonde hair,
my blue eyes. I am immediately attracted
to your sense of humor, your dance moves.
We wed outside, with the Atlantic Ocean
as one of our guests. We move to Shanghai
to live and work. We inhale Bali air, soak
up Thai sunshine. In Xi'an, we marvel
at the soldiers, and visit Ming tombs. We
watch soccer games in France and Korea,
cruise the Nile and the Cyclades. We hike
amid tall pines in the woods, hang pictures
on the walls of our Stateside cottage,
arrange our Asian treasures. Our luggage
becomes battered, our passports fat.

You will not get a terminal diagnosis. I will not
bake chocolate chip cookies or spoon-feed
you ice cream. My summers won't be spent
at your bedside. You won't lose your ability
to walk, talk, or remember. Your only trip
won't be in a wheelchair. You will mark in red
the route we drive in Australia. You will put
the zoom lens on the camera to capture the
beauty of the inner passage in Alaska. We will
teach sixth graders overseas and still save
enough money to retire at sixty. We will sit
on the back deck, drink cocktails, hold each
other's wrinkled, age-spotted hands, and with
our fading eyesight, we will watch the sun
flicker between the leaves as it goes down.

Far Removed

I'm near, yet I feel isolated, as if I
am sitting on one side of a river bank

and you are on the other. There's no boat
to cross the water of this ever widening

river of disease. No matter how far
I stretch my arms, they can't reach you.

I feel wrenched away from you,
as if a sudden wind has torqued me miles

and miles into another life, to this island
where my other self, my unpartnered persona,

lives and works and marks the calendar,
a day at a time, until the next vacation

when my heart is side by side with yours,
when I can rest my hand on your bony chest,

kiss your cheek, when all I can do is sit and wait
and gaze at this river's reflection of who we used to be.

April Fools

Seven years ago
I thought you
were dying,
right there
on the white nubby
couch, nonsense
syllables uttered
from your mouth
as saliva leaked
out of its corners, eyes
glazed, fixed on some
point in the distance.

When the attendees
arrived to take you
to the hospital, your
brain seized, body
flailed, red-faced,
resisted the touch
of their hands,
as you had drawn
away from mine
when I tried to soothe
your fears, bring
you back to me.

April 1, 2005, but this
was no joke, no prank
you were pulling. I
can still hear
the sirens screech,
feel the bumpy ride
we took, are still
taking.

Evanescence

Your illness wrecks me
the way a tornado wrecks
a house. I try to dodge
bits of debris the way
a combat soldier dodges
bullets. Work is my cover
where I hide behind
a smile, and gird myself
with poetry. Sometimes
I emerge from this shelter,
pick through the fragments
of our former life, and watch
as our happiness dissipates
the way smoke dissipates
in a swirl of wind, my hands
trying to keep hold of a wisp.

Winter Walk

It is a gin tonic night,
clear and clean,
crisp with a hint of pine.

I walk through the woods
this December, new snow
not yet delivered.

I long for it—the placid,
obliterating cover, untread
upon by my past.

Cold air, a companion
keeps my pace, keeps
me looking forward,

no turning back
to get lost in a flurry
of painful memories

watching you
get buried under
a drift of disease.

A shower of moonlight
rains on my back
as I journey on.

The Unpartnered Wife

Like a broken pair
One missing or beyond repair
The unpartnered wife
Married but with a single life
De facto widow
Grieving in limbo

What I Carry

Every time I leave
your bedside to return
to work on an island
you and I planned
to explore, every time
you can't answer
my questions on the phone
because the virus
has silenced your voice,
every time someone asks
me where I'm going
for break and I say
home to you, every time
I explain those letters, *PML:*
Progressive
Multifocal
Leukoencephalopathy,
to our friends and your
family, who should
remember this disease
that robs you from our lives,
every time, I keep each hurt
hidden beneath my skin,
pushing it deep inside
its own pocket of grief.

If Only He Could Say

I'm not in pain,
although my body is stiff.
Dinner was a bit dry,
certainly not up to your standard.
No visitors today,
everyone's busy or has the flu.
No, I'm not interested in listening to a movie.
All the nurses treat me just fine,
very kind in fact.
Got up in my chair for lunch today.
It only hurt a little while in the sling.
It felt good to get out of that bed.
You should have heard the birds at the feeder.
They must have put out new food.
I know how much you love birds.
I wish I could see them.
Yes, my roommate is still watching *The Mummy*.
No, I forgot to turn on the hockey.
I always liked the Canadiens.
Next week I'll remember.
So when are you coming home sweetheart?
Can't wait to see you.
Maybe you can make me some baked spaghetti.
I miss that.
And we can listen to Buffet,
and talk about our old sailboat,
and Chesterfield,
that Thanksgiving we took him out
and he wouldn't relieve himself
until the last day heading home.
Such a good dog.
The nurse is here with medicine.
Yes, the pretty one.
Will you call me tomorrow?
Talk to you then.
I love you.

My Baby

Washing your hair,
careful not to get shampoo
in your eyes,
you becoming the baby
that neither of us
ever wanted.

Brushing your teeth,
so difficult
to get you
to open your mouth
so the brush
fits in:
swishing,
spitting,
afterward,
almost a game.

Feeding you,
trying to encourage
you to eat,
while secretly hoping
you refuse,
so this nightmare
will end.

This nightmare
that strips away
your dignity.
If you were cognizant enough
to protest you would have
ended it yourself.

But the nightmare continues:
washing,
brushing,
feeding.

Close

I am looking
into a near empty
bottle, waiting
for the last
viscous drops
to let go
of its vessel.

Corralled

With a spin and a snap,
the braided loop traps
the unsuspecting calf,
its eyes wide, frightened
by the gripping of the rope,
which tightens around its legs
with every tug, immobilizing

as my devotion to you, my love,
which captures and holds me.
Forced to watch you slip away,
there's no going back, no moving
on. Confined to the present,
I'm left struggling for release.

Threshold

Death is an acquaintance who knocks
on my door at awkward hours, who rouses
me from my status quo stupor to look
into hollow, haunted eyes. It wants to settle
in, to fill my closet with drab dresses
that hang heavy on the rod. It longs
to crowd my life with its presence, to sleep
in my bed, to sit at my kitchen table.
I struggle with this interloper, show
it my back. I resist what it proffers: relief
from watching you search for the words
that don't come, release from bedside vigils;
respite from wakeful nights spent waiting
the arrival of this unwanted guest.

Tortured Sonnet

This disease locks us in its hateful snare.
Your diagnosis is a certainty,
which leaves me to wait hopeless with despair
and dread of its eventuality.
The anguished drip of torment like a clock,
so steady it maintains a constant beat,
that marks the time until this thought is not,
a thought at all, but is reality.
When worry's prodding tines no longer pierce
my psyche with incessant questioning,
when fate gives answers as to what will be,
and the rising of your chest with air has ceased,
when Earthly shackles loose their tightening,
the trap will open; death will set us free.

Satisfied

After you were sick,
you said you just wanted
to reach 50.
As long as you made it
to 50, you said,
the rest would be gravy.
Gravy, you said,
because you had already
feasted on the flesh
of a bloody steak,
years struggling for a job
you loved, finally finding
it teaching overseas;
Swallowed whole the mashed
potatoes with their pools
of butter, you and me hiking
on The Great Wall,
crouching in a dank
Egyptian pyramid, basking
in Bali's kaleidoscopic warmth;
Crunched down on Romaine
leaves bobbing with tomatoes,
coaching and playing soccer, taping
your ankles for extra strength;
Torn into the oven hot cloverleaf
dinner roll, ingesting its good fortune
with loyal friends, a devoted wife;
Tipped back glass after rocks glass
of Johnny Walker Black, leaving
the satisfied taste of life
in your mouth.

Future Memories

Because you say you can't wait
three hours to see my blue eyes
sparkle, to steep in my *Deep Red* scent
that lingers beneath my ears, emanates
from my breasts, you come home early,

put your lips on my neck, knowing
just where to kiss. I tingle. Chills streak
to my thighs. I nuzzle your broad shoulders,
rake my fingers through the wavy hair
that grazes your nape. You shiver
like you always do when I touch you there.

The years haven't diluted this desire
to hold onto each other, to give
what is needed. I want us
to make this memory
again and again.

What the Brain Knows

He touches my arm twice as he sits beside
me in the backseat of the cab on the short

ride from school to Din Tai Fung, while I
tell him about James, about how poetry

saved me, saves me now. In the restaurant,
I sit next to him in the booth, across

from the others who chat about books,
music, wives who speak foreign languages.

He touches my arm three times
during dinner, stacks of bamboo steamers

before us. We aren't intimates, he and I,
have only just met, though from reading

his books, I know him: his childhood,
his writing muses, his marriages. His touches

cause an explosion of recognition in my brain
like when I hear a word of Mandarin I understand.

I don't go downtown with the group,
choose to go home instead, don't exchange

addresses or emails with him, don't promise
to send him my writing. We don't hug

goodbye. Outside, I open my umbrella
and walk home in the rain.

So Much for Being Good

What has it gotten me?
White hair, wrinkles,
high cholesterol, high blood
pressure, a sick and dying
husband who can't tell me
he loves the way my eyes
sparkle or did sparkle before
I was weary with worry
and heavy with work.
Can't kiss me on the lips
or touch my breasts.
Can only solicit feelings
of motherly love, pity
from me now. Devotion
to duty. So fuck sobriety.
To hell with exercise. It's pizza
for breakfast. Gin and tonic
for dinner. Elastic waist
pants. Grasshopper shoes.
Leave school early. Eat
buttery popcorn at a skin
flick on a Monday afternoon.
How much worse can it get?
I look up to see lightning
just before it fades to black?

The Day for Lovers

Walking home alone
trying to decide

what to have for dinner
tonight—the night

set aside for romantic
candlelit meals. A pint

of tiramisu Haagen Daz?
Both layers of chocolates

in a red heart-shaped box?
Perhaps a bag of popcorn

while watching *The Holiday*?
Rather than wallow in the fact

that you are there
and I am here,

and your brain disease
keeps you from sending

me Valentine's wishes,
I will remember

that Valentine's Day
when your friend, the chef,

cooked us a gourmet meal
of blackened mahi mahi

and rice pilaf in our very own
kitchen. I will count

myself lucky. I will think
back to all of the evenings

we shared listening to music
on our back deck,

while the stars lit up
the black sky.

Happy Hour

On the deck,
warm diagonals
slash brown boards
in colorful angles,
as we sip
our cocktails:
yours amber,
mine clear.
Late afternoon
listening to Neil Young,
his, the only angst
in the atmosphere
on this summer day.
The clinking sound
of ice against glass
prompts me to action;
I refresh our drinks.
Two months times
two summers of bliss,
until too soon,
disease casts its shadow
upon our happy hour,
causing your glass
to tumble and break,
shattering our lives,
leaving jagged shards of it,
tiny bits of memory
that sparkle like crystals,
that wedge into my flesh,
pricking my psyche
with the past.

Tapestry

over, under
woof, warp
two threads strong
youth, lust, love
orange and blue on the color wheel
sails full of Florida air
cottage nestled in tall pines
glass rings on the arms
of the Adirondack deck chairs
twin LaZy Boys bookend the fireplace
scuffed Samsonites by the front door
fat passports, wallets stuffed with foreign currency
photo albums on the coffee table
illness, tension, snap
folders of lesion films, CT scans blanket the desk
baskets of prescription bottles by the sink
behind the door a cane, fold-up walker
portable wheelchair, purple sling
swinging from a Vanderlift
single bolster bed, stained white sheets
under, under
warp, warp
one thread stretches

Still

Alone in this house.
Only the birds' trilling
breaks the silence.

Rhododendrons grow
over the deck rails
while goatsrue invades

the front yard. A stellar
jay nurtures its young
in the nest it built

by the door. The loose
twigs scrape when I open
it to leave what was our house,

to go to you in your hospital
bed. I hold your hand. I watch
you sleep. Eyes matted shut,

thin limbs on a cloud of pillows,
thin lips quiver but utter no sound,
only your chest rises, falls.

Leaving Me

And when I see
your face,
    with dim eyes
    and slackened jaw,
I will know you are gone.

The last glimmer
of you,
    will have vanished,
    leaving me,
a bereft vessel.

Gone

Locked in?
Trapped?
Perhaps,
or
maybe
you
escaped
before
dignity
deserted
you.

One More Day

for Susan

Now when I come to work, I don't
notice the smell. Smoking helps.
It is for the visitors I spray the room
after I change a brief, slide open a window
to flush the stench of feces that thickens
the air, mingles with the odor of aging flesh,
urine, baby powder, and sweat, cloaked
in cinnamon or *Fresh Summer Breeze*. This smell
that tells me their organs still function,
still produce, despite their age, despite
their infirmity.

I do what family can't or won't. Sometimes,
the wife helps, but usually it is just me
rolling and turning, pulling a slackened body
up in bed, brushing teeth in a resistant mouth,
mindful of my knuckles. I comb and fuss
with hair, shave chins, scratch backs. I cut meat,
stir soup, tempt tired taste buds with ice cream
and root beer floats. I explain how busy their son
is, hold up the grandbaby's photo so they can see
its new teeth.

Tuesday is Bingo. A parade of stooped back
women roll and walker themselves down the hall
to the living room. I give their chairs a push,
and wish them good luck as they pass by. Every
Friday afternoon is Happy Hour. I wheel those
who can't get there on their own to the dining
room to listen to the accordion player squeeze
out songs of their youth. I smile as I watch
them drink beer, eat snacks, laugh and sing,
relive good times.

At lunch, I drink my diet Pepsi, smoke
two cigarettes, stand outside by my open
car door. I look at the gray clouds, dream
of vacation in Palm Springs, where the sun
is ever present on my skin. Then I throw the empty
bottle into the back seat, take a final puff,
smash the butt with my foot, and head inside
for last rounds.

Before My Eyes

The whoosh of air
inflates your mattress,
the one that prevents

bed sores, while Zevon
sings, "Dad get me out
of this." Your lip curls,

your eyes flash open
as if you recognize
something—you can't say

what, as if vapors
rise up out of the speaker,
ethereal tentacles reaching

into your brain, excavating
your memories buried
beneath disease.

Drinking beer, the mugs' frost
steams, then disappears
in the Key West heat--

Driving home, the rear view
streaks red and purple,
as the Atlantic swallows the sun--

In Bali with the camera
set, racing to get in the shot
before the shutter clicks--

Another Northwest summer day,
reading on the back deck,
watching ice in your glass melt--

Lying in your hospital bed,
nurses chatter around you,
charting your weight less and less--

The song ends and I,
touch your face.

Feed Your Head

"A mind is a terrible thing to waste."
"A wasting mind is a terrible thing."

You who have spent your time
traversing the gray and white terrain,
exploring its topography,
probing its deep canyons,
charting unknown regions,
surveying hemispheres right and left,
uncovering the long and short of it,
you encephaloexplorers,
you neurocartographers,
excavate the theory and unfurl the map
that explains to me how it is that my husband
can't tell me what he just ate for lunch,
what year it is, whether or not he had a bath;
can't recall friends of ten years,
the places we visited, his beloved dog,
what his father said every Tuesday,
doesn't remember how to walk,
when to swallow, but knows
what the dormouse said.

Voice

Today you failed to know my voice,
Even though I said, "It's me, your wife."
They're gone—the short and long memories
To the remote edges of your brain,
That puts you in this frail state,
And renders me heartbroken.

I held my tears though heartbroken,
Not wanting despair to show in my voice,
Or to upset your docile state.
It's all a part of being a wife,
To fret about you and your brain,
And to refresh your memories.

I talk of our days to jog your memories,
Thinking my words will awaken your brain.
But you give no sign, leaving me heartbroken.
I yearn for something in my voice,
To remind you I'm your wife,
As you lie far from me in a distant state.

You're suspended in a limbo state,
Only here in this instant with no memories,
No past nor future not even a wife.
If you understood you'd be heartbroken.
You rarely speak, you cannot voice
What feelings there are in your brain.

Shrinking in size your once robust brain,
Reducing your body to this slackened state.
Daily I try to reach you with my voice,
But too soon it's faded with your memories,
And all I can do is wait heartbroken,
Trying my best to be a loyal wife.

For twenty years I've been your wife,
And for longer I've admired your brain.
Without you near, I'm left to live heartbroken.
Despairing in this solitary state,
With only my sweet memories
Of you, and the infrequent sound of your voice.

Tomorrow I hope you know my voice as the one belonging to your wife,
Restoring the memory of me in your brain,
So together we can enjoy a contented state, and for a while not be heartbroken.

Like a Dream

From the airport taxi the view is a green blur as we race past rice paddies, steps cut precisely into Earth angled against a sky so blue it hurts our eyes. The sun seems bigger here as we enter the mystical world of daily temple offerings carried by silk-sashed beauties who behind each ear sprout an intricately designed flower in shocking pink, flaming orange, blood red, some with tongues protruding as if licking the air. For here the air is delicious, steeped in clove, ginger, nutmeg, frangipani, lily, lotus, and the fecund odor of Bali's dirt. We gobble up as much of it as we can.

you are you again
inside this kaleidoscope
of my memories

Remaining Faithful

My dreams are filled with lovers
from my past, before you, strong
blonde men who cup my breasts
in their hands. I wake to the heat
of it, try to hold that warmth
between my chest and the sheet,
but it dissipates as does this dream.
Wisps of past intimacies swirl
around my drowsy mind: wet
arms and legs entangled, grasp
for purchase in salt water,
waves slap in reply to hip thrusts.
I try to summon the dream,
to finish what was started. Awake,
I have only illness-tempered
memories of our naked bodies
in the shower, you holding onto
me for balance as I wash between
your legs, a perfunctory touch,
inadequate sustenance
for this gnawing hunger
you can no longer feed.

Is Sleep Not Rehearsal

for death as I lie supine,
eyes shuttered, inert
for hours in a thought-
less void, devoid of pain
or pleasure? Sometimes
I float heavenward,
streaks of bright
sunshine in a green
glade, wafts of violets,
the weight of lips on lips,
a gush of warmth.
Still other times
I watch as you fall
backward off a deck,
me reaching, reaching,
but never catching
you in this hell where
terror clogs my throat,
making mute my screams
until I wake up and know
we live in purgatory.
No performance today.

What I Hold Onto

Your Glacier National Park sweatshirt,
the one you bought just before we moved
to Washington, your faded gray
and brown plaid flannel shirt you wore
over everything when the temperatures plunged
during Key West winters, these same shirts I wear
sitting on our deck, their arms embracing me on chill
summer nights, XXLs that barely contained your girth
then, items of clothing I couldn't give to the homeless
shelter, even though at one hundred thirty-seven
pounds, you'd drown in them.

The words of writers whose books I stack around me
to forge sea walls when waves of grief
begin to slosh. "…what we love is not to be held…"
Mary Oliver says; advice from Joan Didion,
none but *magical thinking* can keep me afloat.
Donald Hall prepares me for the afterdeath
with his gallery of Janes; in our living room stands
your photo gallery: the young you in bathing trunks,
the middle-aged you in your Jeep, the healthy you
on the Great Wall of China, and even now, the sick
but smiling you in your wheelchair.

Rings with memories that anchor me, the solitary
pearl that celebrates our ten years living
in Shanghai, the aquamarine stone you brought back
from your Habitat for Humanity trip to Sri Lanka,
wedding bands our jeweler in Key West crafted
from your mother's old gold pieces--
mine with its rubies and diamonds, yours octagonal,
adorned with one square of jade; how it would swim
on your slack finger now, how it hangs on a chain
around my neck like a life preserver.

Rise Up

There are still
places we need
to see: Australia's outback,
Alaska's Inner Passage,
Karst formations in Viet Nam,
Brazil's beaches.

Rise up
and get another dog
to walk in the woods,
to swim in the creek,
to train like you did
with Chesterfield.

Choose one of the six empty
chairs at our dining room
table and eat. I'll make
your favorites: baked spaghetti,
garlic bread, cheesecake for dessert.

Afterward, we can sit
by the fire, me in my
LaZy boy, you in yours.
You can read the newspaper,
drink Scotch on the rocks.
Or we can listen to Neil Young,
on the deck in our Adirondack chairs.

When night descends, come
into the bedroom, throw off
the books filling up your side
of our King size bed, and put
your arm around me.

Defy this disease that renders
you motionless, mute, place
your thin frail legs on the floor,
push off that hospital bed
with a shout, and rise up,
won't you?

The Art of Healing

Involves time, at least
100 days for my sprained
knee a Taiwanese friend
says. And so I limp a bit
as I walk to work knowing
someday soon it will once
again be strong enough to trust.
How much time does an injured
heart need to heal? This organ
that can't rest as it throbs
in my chest, can't be elevated
or iced as it loves despite
the pain it squeezes through
valves with each lub, no brace
to support it with each dub.
What therapy should I take
to lessen the ache, reduce
the inflammation being away
from you causes? What balm
or poultice can I apply to soothe
my hobbled heart? How long
before it too will be strong
enough to trust?

Exposed

Unlike the rings of a tree--hidden beneath the bark, the years not revealed until death--my wrinkles are there for all to see. Each tied to a memory. This one across my forehead that I try to hide with bangs? This trench carved into my facial landscape? You created that one with years of worry about what was happening to you when your legs wouldn't obey your brain; when your eyes saw images that only you could see; your words seeming sensical to you but nonsense to me. One neurologist visit after the other, pinpricks to the bottoms of your feet, finger to nose and back to the doctor's finger, tests you failed time after time. MRI becoming routine, the stillness of your body in stark contrast to the booming knocks of the magnet.

That day in the living room, we were drinking cocktails. Your eyes glazed. Drool dribbled down your chin. I sat with you waiting for help to arrive, hoping you'd let me touch your knee. You reared back like a panicked animal. They took you, strapping you into the ambulance, bouncing up over the sidewalk, running stoplights, the siren blaring. In the emergency room I signed papers, holding back my tears, while you bucked under the straps of the CT machine, as our friend, Dean, tried to tame you with his sweet, tender lullabies. My trench widening with every IV they stuck in your arm—so many failed attempts to raise a vein—your arms purple and pocked—the furrows deepening with each doctor's voice that couldn't reassure me.

You are still here, etching lines in my face when you won't take my calls at the nursing home, won't take your medicine, spitting it out like a child, when they tell me you've lost another ten pounds, when you cry over *Twister* because you can't distinguish fantasy from reality, tears gliding down your smooth face. Your brain disease erasing all trace of worry like a viral Botox. You looking younger than your years, more handsome than ever, leaving my face to look my years plus yours, exposing the rings of my tree, not waiting until death to tell my story.